The Top Twenty Books and Documentaries
Black Folks Must Study

By Xavier James

If you watch one documentary this year make sure it's one of these:

1. <u>African History v/s Biblical Myth-</u> One of Ashra Kwesi's best presentations. He leaves you with overwhelming evidence and documentation to back it up. In this fascinating lecture/documentary, Kwesi leaves no stone unturned and removes any doubt about the origin of Christianity.

a.) ***<u>The Naked Truth-</u>*** A lot of "African-Americans" won't believe anything unless its coming from a white man. So, let them tell you what a lot of white folks have known for centuries

.

b.)*<u>Zeitgeist-</u>* Documentary in three parts uncovering unbelievable lies and propaganda about religion, politics and power; a must see!

2. *<u>Maafa 21: 21st Century Genocide-</u>* You're going to be shocked to find out what the number one killer of black folks in America is. You'll also be shocked to find out who's behind it all.

<u>a.) John Hopkins Hospital; a history of genocide against blacks</u>- Two dynamic young brothers step forward and present miles of evidence documenting the atrocities committed and hidden by John Hopkins hospital and University. It could literally save your life!

3. _Black Inventors and their Patents-_ Its not just hearsay they actually owned the patents. Once you see and hear their stories it will become clear why your teacher had to lie to you.

4. _The Black Wall Street-_ This documentary reveals another one of white Americas closely guarded secrets; the malicious bombing and meticulous cover up of an all black economic empire in Tulsa Oklahoma.

5. _Goodbye Uncle Tom-_ This unbelievable docu-drama was banned in America since 1973. If you think violence erupted when Roots and Mississippi Burning came out, imagine what would have happened if Black folks had seen this. The French directors used the actual diaries, captains logs, articles and books of that era to bring your slave masters back to life. Unbelievable!

a.) _500 Years Later-_ This well guided and directed documentary details the 500 years since the European kidnappings and enslavement. It also covers myths, lies and propaganda as well as extends a road map for the future. It's great inspirational documentary for us all.

6. _Ethnic Notions-_ Did you ever wonder where the watermelon eating 'Coon' and 'Sambo' came from? Hosted by Ester Rolle (Good Times) this documentary examines how early the white racist media took control of black images and tried to destroy them.

7. ***Africans in America before Columbus-*** This hard to find underground documentary includes interviews and insight from Dr. John Henrik Clark, Dr. Ivan Van Sertima And Dr. Yosef ben-Jochannan among others.

8. ***How to De-Activate the Willie Lynch Chip-*** Dr. Ray Hagins explains the Willie Lynch Syndrome and how to break it. Excellent lecture.

9. ***The Isis Papers-*** Dr. Frances Cress Welsing puts some of her groundbreaking book into a lecture. The trained and certified psychiatrist analyzes the collective patterns of racism and what makes white America tick.

10. ***Post Traumatic Slave Syndrome-*** Following in the path blazed by Dr. Welsing, Dr. Joy Degreary also puts her groundbreaking book into a lecture to help us see patterns of thought and actions that has to be diagnosed in order to be cured.

11. ***Powernomics: The National Plan to Empower Black America-*** is a five-year plan to make Black America a prosperous and empowered race that is self-sufficient and competitive as a group.

12. ***The Death of Black America: Health Matters-*** Indeed health does matter. You're health is all you've got. And Dr. Laila Afrika gives us a sobering look at what we've been putting into our bodies and how its slowly but surely killing us.

a.) _You're Leaders Betrayed You: The Cure for Cancer, Sickle Cell and A.I.D.S-_ Dr. Sebi, *the world* renowned healer has cured several ailments with his Electric Cell Food. Reversing illnesses such as : Cancer, Herpes, H.I.V, Diabetes, Aids, High Blood Pressure, Blindness, Fibroids etc. Believe it or not; everything is worth a try when you're out of options.

13. _The African Origin of Civilization and Spiritual Concepts-_ Yet Another excellent Ashra Kwezi joint. Kwezi takes us back to where it all began and shows documented proof (evidence) of where theology and spiritual concepts started.

14. _Marcus Garvey-_ An in depth documentary about the man who started the biggest, organized black power movement in America.

a.) _Malcolm X-_ Yeah, the Spike Lee Joint.
b.) _Emit Till; The Untold Story-_ Do you want to know what really sparked the Civil rights Movement? Well it wasn't Rosa Parks.

c.) _Unforgivable Blackness: The Rise and Fall of Jack Johnson-_ The one black man in America who could not be lynched. Excellent documentary about the greatest boxer of all time.

15. _The Korean Takeover-_ Just how did the Asians manage to keep blacks on economic lock down?

a.) *Good Hair*- Chris Rock's satirical look at Black women and their hair.

16. *It's a Dam Shame: Homosexuality in Hip-Hop-* This here documentary goes straight for the jugular!

17. *Dr. Khalid Muhammad on Donahue/Dr. Francis Cress Welsing on Donahue-* If you want to see warrior - scholars in action check them out. They're both battling racism on the world stage...two different styles ...one result; controversy and truth.

18. *John Henrik Clarke - A Great and Mighty Walk* - I'm a big fan of this master teacher and this video chronicles the life and times of the noted African-American historian, scholar and Pan-African activist John Henrik Clarke (1915-1998).

19. *Professor Griff Raw Uncut Exposing The Music Industry/Hollywood-* Professor Griff DVD exposing mind control, the music Industry, Hollywood and Illuminati members.

a.) *Collapse-*A documentary on Michael Ruppert, a police officer turned independent reporter who predicted the current financial crisis in his self-published newsletter, 'From the Wilderness'. Ruppert was also the guy who told on the CIA drug rings and said his former LAPD *Colleague's* killed Rapper Biggie Smalls. Contains a lot of good info.

20. *The Spook Who Sat By The Door-*

THE TOP TEN NON-FICTION (HISTORY) BOOKS BLACK FOLKS MUST READ

IF YOU READ ONE BOOK THIS YEAR MAKE SURE IT'S ONE OF THESE!

<u>10. The Book of Coming Forth By Day by Your African Ancestors-</u> Why read a book that's thousands of years old? Because most of you have been reading pieces of it your entire life without even knowing it. Of course you're not going to find the actual papyrus, but find it online and dig in.

<u>b.) Ancient Egypt: The light of the World by Gerald Massey 1907 and 2007 General Books LLC.</u> Massey interprets and breaks down the origin of long held religious beliefs, rituals and practices to reveal that the African- Egyptians gave God consciousness to the world; proves where 95% of Christianity and other religions originated from.

<u>9.) The Destruction of Black Civilization: Great Issues of Race Between 4500 B.C. And 2000 A.D. by Chancellor Williams 1987 Third World Press-</u> Dr. Williams spent 16 years of research (mostly on the African continent itself) to compile what is the most comprehensive black -African-American history book in existence today. Thousands of hidden facts and references reiterate this book should be in schools across this country. And to his credit he even offers a plan of action.

<u>8.) The African Origin of Civilization: Myth or Reality by Cheikh Anta Diop 1974-</u> Diop's work is truly fascinating. His field research and melanin test of "mummies" blows the lid off white racist myths. Diop uses science and documentation to help restore Africans to their rightful place in history.

b.)<u>We the Black Jews: Witness to the ' White Jewish Race' Myth, Vol. 1 and 2 by Yosef A.A. Ben-Jochannan 1989 Lawrence Hill Books.-</u> Well researched and filled with references, Dr. Ben puts the spotlight back on the fraud of the century by showing western scholarship for what it vastly contains; fabrication and embellishment. The book includes well illustrated documentation that's impossible to dispute.

c.)<u>The Secret Relationship Between Blacks and Jews by The Nation of Islam 1991.-</u> Four words: Amazing, enlightening, horrific and indisputable. The Jews themselves provide the evidence that will leave you in shock. Their hatred and domination of Blacks is irrefutable. A definite must read!

d.)<u>The Jewish Onslaught by Tony Martin 1993 Majority Press.-</u> How can someone be anti-Semetic if they're merely repeating what you said? Jews who tried to keep their racism hidden, were outed, causing a hysterical backlash and hostility towards Martin.

7. <u>Stolen Legacy: Greek Philosophy is Stolen Egyptian Philosophy by George GM James 1954 and 2002 African American Images.-</u> The first book ever banned on college campuses…why? James opened the flood gate for fact finding on ancient Greece. So controversial and groundbreaking James was killed for the information he revealed inside.

b.)<u>Black Athena: The Afro-asiatic Roots of Classical Civilization (The Fabrication of Ancient Greece, 1785-1985) by Martin Bernal 1991 Rutgers University</u>

Press.- This broad work details the theft, fraud and plagiarisms of so called Greek philosophy; Greek philosophy does not exist.

c.)They Came Before Columbus by Dr. Ivan Van Sertima 1976 Random House.- Brilliant work, research and documentation encapsulate the fact that Africans were in the Americas long before Columbus.

6.) The Mis-Education of the Negro by Carter G. Woodson 1933 and 1990 Africa World Press.- Almost 80 years and Dr. Woodson's observations and analysis are still relevant today.

5.) 100 Amazing Facts About the Negro With Complete Proof by J.A. Rogers 1952 and 1995 Helga M. Rogers Publisher. -Self explanatory; get the book and be amazed!

4.) Homosexuality and the Effiminization of Afrikan Males by Mwalimu K. Bomani Baruti 2003 by Akoben House.- Baruti's ten years of research yields the most comprehensive work on homosexuality in existence today. From its origins in Europe to it political stranglehold on America, Baruti shows the uninterrupted continuum of sexual perversion and its unparallel effects on people of African descent everywhere.

3.) Dirt: A social history as seen through the uses and abuses of dirt by Terrence McLaughlin 1988 Dorsett Press.- You have to learn something about European history outside the scope of what you've been fed. This book reveals the true European history that's been hidden for years. It contradicts the glitz and glamour your teachers and Hollywood presented as facts.

2.) <u>Post Traumatic Slave Syndrome: Americas Legacy of Enduring Injury and Healing by Dr. Joy Leary 2005 Uptone Press.</u> -Once again, a hard hitting, long overdue examination of the behaviors that have permanently fragmented black families and kept a psychological rope around our necks. The damage done from slavery was not just economic or physical; it was deeply psychologically traumatic, causing each generation since to pass that trauma down. How do blacks collectively heal from slavery and move forward? Do whites play a substantial role in this healing process? Dr. leary provides the definitive answer to both.

1.) <u>The Isis Papers: The Keys to the Colors by Dr. Francis Cress Welsing 1991 Third World Press.</u> - Dr. Welsing answers the tough questions no one wants to tackle. She uncovers and analyzes the collective white behavior and why their behavior patterns can only destroy Black life not just in America but around the world. She explains the origins of the numerous problems that have plagued Blacks globally for centuries. For years the symptoms are easy to see, however Dr. Welsing exposes the actual disease: racism (white Supremacy). Most importantly, she offers well thought out, interesting solutions.

"UNTIL YOU UNDERSTAND RACISM (WHITE SUPREMACY) EVERYTHING ELSE WILL ONLY CONFUSE YOU." -*Neely Fuller*

ADDITIONAL READING:

*Anything with the name JOHN HENRIK CLARKE on it; Yes he was that good!

*The United-Independent Compensatory Code/System/Concept by Neely Fuller, Jr.

*The HISTORY of the MOORISH EMPIRE in EUROPE and SPAIN (different authors, volumes and publishers)

*The GOSPEL of ENOCH

*The African Origins of the Jewish People/The Moses Mystery by Gary Greenberg

*Chosen People From the Caucus Mountains by Michael Bradley

*Columbus' Captain's Log/Journal (his first and second voyage)

Also by Xavier James:

Eugenics, Sterilization and Planned Parenthood by Xavier James

The Top 5 Most Ratchet Television Shows That Hurt Black America

Copyright © 2015 by Xavier James

The Top 5 Most Ratchet Television Shows That Hurt Black America

By Xavier James

Do you remember the movie "A Soldier's Story?" It was one of Denzel Washington's first movies and one of my favorites. Adolph Caesar played a sergeant who hated coons so much it drove him over the edge. Well, I feel just like him every time I see one of these bootlicking, buck-dancing, NEGROES pop up on television.

meanwhile.......

These 5 shows contributed to the dumbing down, the blatant ignorance and outright spectacle that has become black American television..

5.)*Flavor of Love*

If the term **"sell out"** means you'll do absolutely anything for money/you sold your soul to the devil/ lost all your moral fiber/ made your family look bad/ made your race look worse/pimp and exploit black women because white men told you too/ then yes Flavor Flav has all the basis covered.

After the first season of 'Flavor of Love' and Flavor Flav still hadn't been banished to Coonsville, the general consensus throughout white Hollywood was that black folks don't get embarrassed; wrong. Buffoons don't get embarrassed; black folks actually do. And believe me there's a difference.

This **VH-1 reality** show was about a washed up hype man from a popular rap group trying to find a wife out of a host of half naked, scandalous, manipulating and manipulated women from around the country. The producers, with Flaver Flavs help of course; pit the women against each other while he pretended to search for the perfect one to marry. The show provided lots of fodder for water cooler conversations and made Flavor Flav the most popular of all the California raisins.

4.)Meet the Browns/House of Payne

Until I saw *'Meet the Browns'* I didn't think it was possible to get that much **'buck dancing'** into one half-hour show. But Tyler Perry did it! He was able (with the help of over 2 million Negroes strong) to bring back stereotypes and set black television back 60 years.

Do you want to know why there are no black dramas, mystery's, game shows, documentaries or detective series on TV and maybe only one or two on cable? *Because of* Tyler Perry and people like him; indirectly of course. Why do you think good shows get cancelled? "Under Covers" starred Boris Kodjoe and Gugu Mbatha-Raw as CIA spies. But thanks to decades of Amos and Andy style comedy no one wanted to believe two black actors could be spies.

If they weren't falling down, farting or calling on Jesus no one wanted to see them. It seems like these days, black folks are only on television to make white folks laugh at them, not with them; there's a difference. The low- brow humor in these black comedies help pave the way for the cancellation and phasing out of anything other then buffoonery. Trust and believe me when I say that the world actually does view you the same way as they see you on television. Now, give yourselves a round of applause!

3.) The Jerry Springer Show

Throughout the 90's *The Jerry Springer Show'* became a household name and a feeding frenzy for homosexuals and gay activists across the country. More Black males "came out of the closet" on The 'Jerry Springer Show' then any other forum in the world. And Jerry Springer was more than happy to laugh, jeer and joke every guest who set foot on his stage- searching for their15 minutes of fame. Most of his black guests were either on the down low, cheating, prostituting or hiding some cross dressing secret. It's a fact, no news was good news if you were on the 'Jerry Springer Show'. Despite that fact there was never a shortage of black folks waiting back stage to give or receive shocking news. For his part Springer was clever at creating a circus atmosphere that culminated in a gladiator environment that literally put guests at each other's throats. But don't worry, at the end of the show Jerry would sit down and give a brief commentary on why his guests had to be exploited. And guess what? It was for their own good.

2.) The Maury Show

When he's not playing guessing games like "is it a man or woman," in which he giggles as transvestites kiss all over him while the audience guesses if they're male or female, Mo-rri (as they call him in the hood) is busy exploiting black folks; most of whom are too ignorant to even know they're being exploited.

While Jerry Springer's raunchy, skanky exploitation seems evenly distributed between both races; Maury's sophisticated brand of exploitation is overwhelmingly black.

His show takes usury to a whole new level. 'The Maury Show' directly targets a black demographic and brings them on the show to makes them appear loose, stupid and 'ghetto'. Of course he does this under the pretense of helping them find their 'baby's daddy.' Unlike Springer who will tell jokes at his guest's expense, Maury will pretend to be concerned even offering; counseling after the show.

And the younger the guest the more he and his producers are able to manipulate and play off of their immaturity. Maury becomes tickled pink every time a black man comes on stage calling the potential mother of his child "hoes, sluts, and bitches."

The high point of his show is when the distraught mother of a child runs from the stage after she finds out the man she thinks fathered her child is actually not the father. For a guy who couldn't make it as a serious journalist Maury Povich was sure able to make black folks take him seriously.

1.) B.E.T.-(Black Entertainment Television)

Literally ruined about two-three generations of black children. At the time, B.E.T. was the only place black folks could turn to and see images of their selves. It was also the one place artists could get their videos and faces seen on television. And knowing this Bob Johnson and company allowed the raunchiest, degrading, ignorant, ghetto images of black life to be showcased like never before in the history of the world.

 From sagging pants and gold chains, to the booty-butt cheeks on young teenage girls; nothing was off limits. And anyone who complained was either hatin' or lacked vision and if you worked for him; fired. Pay-offs, kickbacks, hosts barely getting paid, homosexual harassment, sexual harassment; it was blacks exploiting blacks at its finest.

 Eventually all the news and education forums were removed until nothing remained but 100% degradation of black women. And money, cars, clothes and hoes for black men. After his grand exploitation of millions of black children, Bob Johnson sold B.E.T. to white folks and left town. However his legacy of teaching consumption, hoochiefied dress and behavior, sagging pants, self devaluation, and a backwards culture still thrives. Thanks B.E.T. and Bob Johnson, thanks.

Honorable Mention:

Most Black Reality TV Shows-Reality shows are serious cash cows for studios. They pay very little to its participants but rake in huge profits. White producers zero in on the biggest idiots and dysfunctional black families in America knowing that they will provide the train wreck people can't take their eyes off.

Take the show 'Real and Chance' for example. They were a cross between Laurel and Hardy and Step- n- fetch it. These two brothers should literally be in a cage somewhere along with Flaver Flav getting bananas tossed at them three times a day.

And it didn't get much better with 'Being Bobby Brown', 'For the Love of Ray J', and 'Basketball Wives'. Who cares about a group of jump- offs that a bunch of washed up basketball players use to date? Yet their classless, shameless, Godless exhibition keeps us all hoping white folks are watching another channel every time they come on. But no, they're watching.

The Source Awards-The most flagrant display of ignorance and stupidity you've ever seen on an awards program. It gave the term ghetto new meaning. The only awards show in history that came with saggin', endless gold teeth, cussin', hollerin' and beat downs. They sure had the vast majority of stereotypes covered that night.

Fresh Prince of Bel- Air- Oh Come on! I understood the 'fish out of water' storyline. But in actuality it was a show about a young black male, who goofs off in school, clowns around all day but succeeds in the end.

Meanwhile Carlton, the other young black male, gets good grades, dresses conservatively and wants to go to college; but he is considered the big joke. Carlton doesn't like rap music. He isn't street savvy and is considered generally unpleasant.

But Will plays basketball, has a smart mouth, is misogynistic, vain, and he wears his hat backwards; he's cool! Carlton can't dance. He is scared of girls and is interested in politics. Will can dance and rap so he gets all the girls.

Do you understand the message that was given to our children? But if I hurt your feelings, you can go have a seat on the shows producer- Quincy Jones' casting couch and tell him all about it.

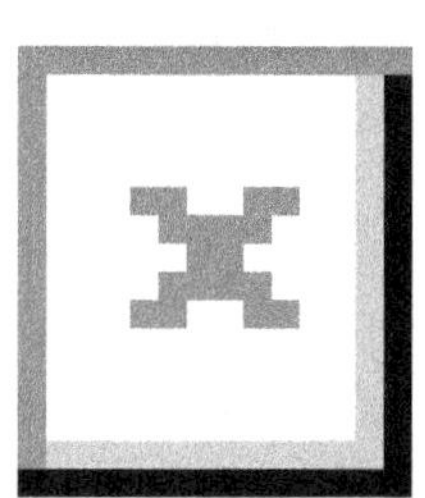

Black Women Declared Most Beautiful on Planet; American Black Woman Most Imitated in the World

By Xavier James

They're bringing out a new Barbie doll with big thighs and ass. Now why are they doing that? Emulating the black woman! Back in the 80's Chic jeans were created to make white women appear to have ass-but that ain't work; all the while white folks were working to destroy the image of black women-go figure.

 Don't go for the Jedi mind trick. Look at all the television anchorwoman on cable; looking, dressing and pumping their lips up to look like you black women. Even the Palestinian hating Joan Rivers and her daughter went from no lips to bubbly lips before she died.

The most imitated woman in the world is the American black woman; she's everything white women inspire to be. It's the same way the white man was sneaking out to the slave quarters to rape the black woman then lie about it; is the same way white women imitate black women and lie about it.

You will never hear them admit it because they're arrogant. Then they go out and throw themselves at every black man they see. When someone's trying to be like you they don't just imitate you, they go get the same man you got, try to have colored children like you and then steal your dialect and slang; to talk like you. Now, am I lying?

Don't let them fuck with your head black woman. When white folks get to the point that they're pumping up the booty of an iconic white symbol like Barbie-BLACK WOMAN- KNOW THAT YOU ARE HANDS DOWN THE SH*T.

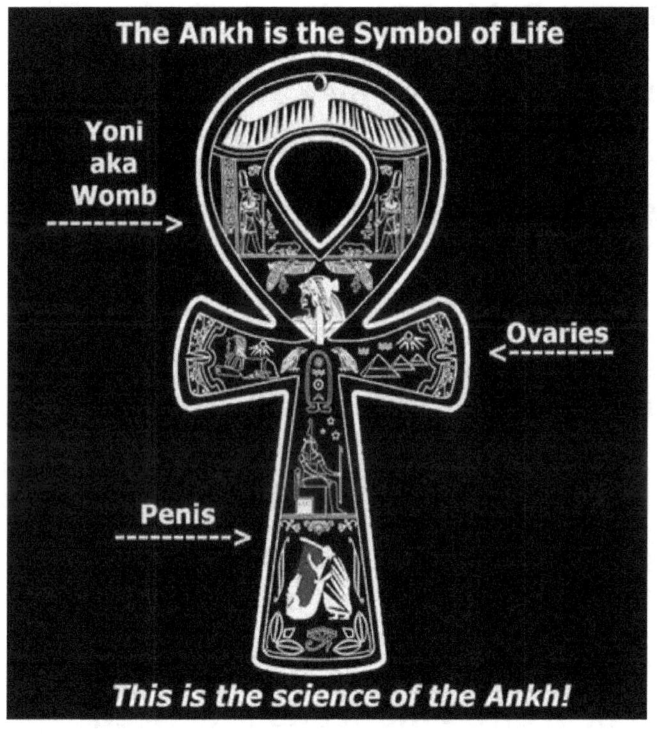

The Ankh is the Symbol of Life
Yoni aka Womb
Ovaries
Penis
This is the science of the Ankh!

Also by Xavier James:

The Secret Behind Dead and Missing Black Americans: Where are they? Who took them and why? by Xavier James
Link: http://amzn.com/B00UB5A126

Exposed: America's Growing Homosexual Factory by Xavier James
Link: http://amzn.com/B00V9P1P5Y

Exposed: The Greatest Identity Theft of All Time: the continued plan to erase Native Americans by Xavier James
Link: http://amzn.com/B00VR3IRHW

Exposed: Are Gifted Schools a Secret Trap for Black Children? by Xavier James
Link: http://amzn.com/B00VJ6A28O

Exposed: White Americans Practiced Cannibalism but Claimed it was the Africans by Xavier James
Link: http://amzn.com/B00VIO8WYS